Bieke Stengos

TRANSMIGRATOR

Poems © by Bieke Stengos 1991
Cover image © by Joan Rentoul 1991
First published by The Private Press 1991
Vocamus Community Publications edition published 2016

ISBN 13: 978-1-928171-32-4 (pbk)
ISBN 13: 978-1-928171-31-7 (ebk)

Vocamus Community Publications
130 Dublin Street, North
Guelph, Ontario, Canada
N1H 4N4

www.vocamus.net

2016

To Ellen, wherever she may be traveling.

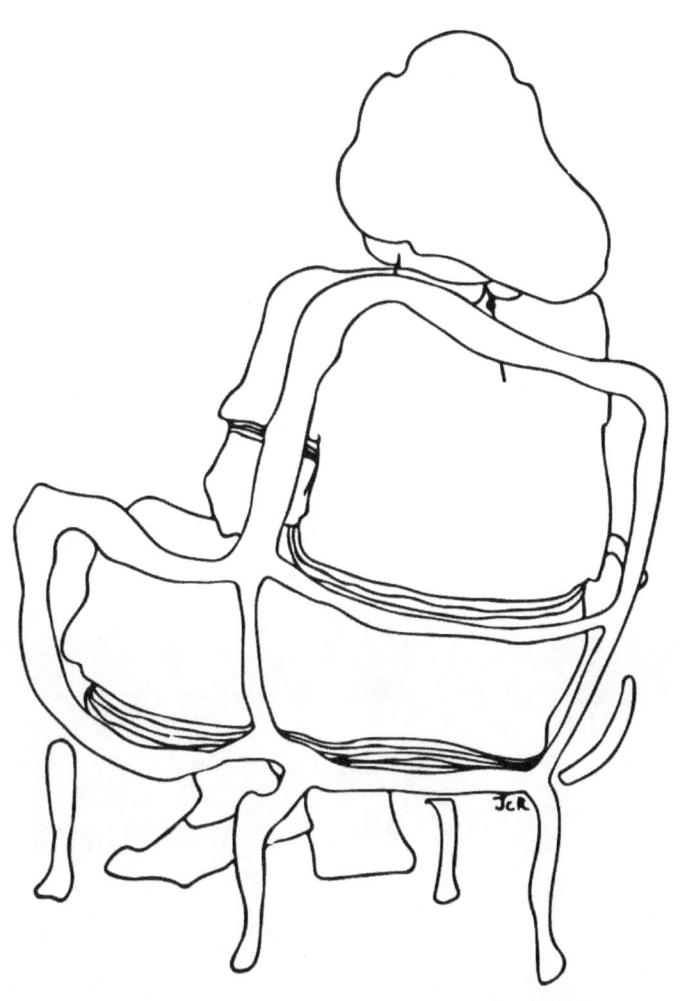

Images of home

When I think of the lowlands
I see bands of mist
like bridal veils
on dank earth freshly turned
and rain clouds
that tumble through
the grey and blue.

And I see you
my mother
with your usual air
propped up in a summer-chair
watching your proprietor
who with nimble fingers
spurns the sinners
to preserve his prized reds
in carefully tended beds.

And then I see no farther
as my eyes scan the border
of your little garden.

When my mother was a young girl...

When my mother was a young girl
they took demure little steps
as they went for Sunday walks
in light summer dresses
and wide hats
to hold back the wind
as it tugged at their skirts.

Delicate whispers
ran from mouth to ear
He kissed me
do you think I am with child?
and
Did you see how he looked at me again
from the other side of the aisle?

Guilt painted a blush on pale cheeks
as glances darted back anxiously
at the stern man
who was walking in earnest thought
while holding the arm
of his gentle wife
in a gesture
of masculine restraint.

The old photograph

Well-behaved delineation
brand the minion eyes
that probe the lines of time
for a reflection in mine
of their tender mobilization

A simple dress of white
a veil of lace
with tumbling flowers
to soften his face
that reveals a faint tremble
at the knees.
His nostrils flare
at the smouldering glare
of wartime lilies
strewn like empty shells
upon her trailing wimple.

These are images of a dark age
that tumble through my brain
as they land broken and forlorn
on a god-forsaken page.

Remembrance day

Her soft brown eyes
doe-shaped
and too young to understand
why they are so painfully aware
of a tired century
do not avert a probing gaze
We never knew about these things, she says.

The other one
older
present at the scene of crime
is visibly shaken
We didn't know it either, back then, she answers.

The age old cop-out of the innocent bystander
falls like a smelly rag
on a plate full of cream puffs
coffee spills from bone china cups
whipping cream
splatters onto the picture
of her young soldier
White chrysanthemums on a chilly grave.

Indigenous state of mind

An accident of birth
recorded
on some paper
is dubious confirmation
of an inalienable claim.

Obliged
because of the right
to be identified
with the piece of land
from which he sprang
man fights.

When winter intrudes on spring

She dances on tiptoes in white lace
while luminous blades of tender grass
deflect off her face
that like the sweet-scented narcissus
stretching eagerly toward the sun
begets its own blameless blaze.

Frost broke from his eyes.

With a sudden dimmer gaze
little fingers blue like the tender bell
reach to cup the crushéd crown
of a frozen flower.
Searing mud-streaked cheeks
suppress the much-needed yell
with amazing power.

Homeland

I choked on your cigarettes
I retched on your booze.
A drunk consumed
I opened wide
to receive you.

The morning after
with pounding pate
I wondered
why of late
the preferred passion
was one of waste.

So I laughed some more
and then I cried
before
I flew away
in nervous haste
through a ring
of fire.

Fading vision

I sit in the sun
with above me
cinder clouds
and around me
sheets of rain
like soiled lace
waving
in the growing
shafts of light
that dim the eye
rather than that they clarify

    I'm all alone
    and I think of you
    behind that veil
    until
    I can no longer
    see you

Spinning

She imprisoned me
blow by silky blow
invading the centre of my being
in ever widening circles
spinning her web
while insisting
that she was
carefully creating me
so that one day
I too could be good
at the game of love.

Amazed
that she taught me so well
I was left to deal
blow by subtle blow
as I watched how
she shrivelled and died.

Now I spin in the wind
on a dragline…

A rose

She offers a rose
He disrobes it
Petal by petal
Until he slips on a thorn

Blood gathers in the cup of her hand

She offers a drink
Blood stains his lips
Red petals stain her dress

A half-plucked rose lies forgotten

Wildfire

You drew juices
from the caverns of a body
juices
fluid
like the longing of life
fluid
from a burning body
running
in the cup of your hand

Then you took me
wild and wilfully
demanding
to still the burning flame

Moisture trickles from tired limbs
drying juice
down the side of a leg
a leg
still trembling
with the flickering and flittering
of fast fading life

Then you left me
wily and gladly
demanding
that I remain cool
and without reproach

Then I cried

My desires
as always ill-conceived
and quickly consumed
scattered
like so many unwanted sparrows
who leave in their haste
to puddles and waste
the stale piece of bread
freshly thrown.

Northern girl

My eyes
      she sighed
      blue
      like these skies
      and my sun-beached hair

She looked deep
into his carefree soul
that stirred
the darkened turmoil
of dank soil
she had hoped to leave behind
as with a single mind
she embraced promises
she knew
he would not keep

Desert seed

Dried up flowers
stir with a last cry
for the gentle breeze
that blows back time
when soft lips
clung to mine
with a thirst for love
which turned to hunger
that with thick moist lips
devoured life.

My heart is a bleeding sun
while petals rub against petals
and rattle in a furious wind
that dashes hopeless seeds
against a barren ground.

Carry on

For Rosemary

Like a queen spreading her lace
she insinuated herself
onto every line
of my tired face.

Far too soon
I fathomed her intentions
as I fell
through the rented web
of life's myriad deceptions.

My clawed hands
leapt from white shreds
as her silken threads
crept like icy breath
within my decaying breast
and feasted on my submissive flesh.

From death to life she came
to take to death again
what she can claim
to leave me
without intervention
to the bones of my contention.

One banquet later

She gets up from chair.
Rich bosom
from tired shoulders
bobs slightly.
She steadies herself.
White table cloth
soaks up drops of champagne.

And then she looked at him
(lover from a distant past)
spilling old wounds
from deepening
darkening lines.

If only you had asked
(she never tells him now
like she never told him then)
instead of taking me so readily
that night
we might not be sitting here
separated by this wide table.

Instead
like a brave soldier
turning old under a tired smile
she raised her glass
and praised
his past performances.

When she sinks down
tears break from triangle eyes
and lips bleed like roses
in a fading autumn sun.

A nightmare

These are the ancient streets
and a carillon peal
to pierce
the leaden sky
like that time
when hip locked to hip
and thighbone to thighbone
we walked
and laughed
in the falling rain.

I sank
mingling tears with drops
that spilled in rivulets
from cracks
between the shining cobble stones
When they told me
    down at the little cafe
    where I confessed
    that I always loved you
how they forced your life
to drain
like rain
into the stinking river.

It must have been the breath of decay
breaking from the sewers
that sent a flood to the river
as it swept over me.

Skopelos

In behind the trellised fence

I see

how they bow eagerly

before a greater majesty

while down below

the roar of the sea

urges me

With trembling knee

I vow once again

like a grateful mariner

to erect my own church

of transacted

tranquillity.

Rite of spring

Rushing sap
like thunder
rolls
to stir tired blood
under crumpled sheets
that with faded colours
of long forgotten dreams
ripple and strain
to shake
the long cold winter.

While trees and children
play the game of spring
she turns
and goes to sleep
again.

You could have spread your wings

Yesterday's eyes
are slow to recognize
the butterflies
that dance
like tired metaphors
before your mind

    You too
    could have spread wide
    that day
    when reaching for the sun
    I tumbled through your light
    which reflected only night

    I deflected swiftly
    while you lingered
    with carefully tucked wing

And now again
a sudden fluttering
or
a drooping eye

Timers: a small cafe

Only last week
the muted din
around simple tables
recalled the time
when I was able
to shed love
like needless skin.
But it was not
until I met your eyes
like open wounds
bleeding lies
that I could define
the true nature
of this illusive time.
    The guitar man
    up on his stage
    croons old songs
    from an easier age
    and
    with heartstrings
    plucked by a minor chord
    I watch how you still cling
    for one moment more
    before you dash
    for the open door.

The seasons of love

My love it seemed
with colours bright
spreading in homeless flight
only left a withered flower.

> I remember clearly, my friend
> that day in July
> a gilded cage and butterfly
> a moment so exquisite
> when love forbidden
> sweet to taste
> could leave no waste
> and collapsed by ivory tower.

When a year later I look into your tears
I am struck down by that extra line,
A confirmation of my hidden fears:
Grief is not exposed before its time.

But come now, friend,
and let us cling to reason:
Seeds only blossom in due season.

Seeing you again

And there was
      blue in blue
      the sea
      and the sky
      with islands
      like floating crystals
      and boats
      like white petals
      adrift

And then there were clouds
      over and above
      and under
      the land
      and the sky

And then there was nothing
      but the noise
      of the fat lady
      in the seat next to mine

And then there was you
      looking bothered
      and shy

And then…

Late love blooming

Your dear face
that myriad of lines
a maze
of love and tears
pains and fear
would take
far more years
than we have left
to burrow through
in the hope
that I may find
that moment in time
when past and future
entwine.

So like the diligent reaper
who takes up pick and hoe
I strive
to turn over
every sigh and every woe
until I am struck
by the gleam in your eye
a youthful yearning
that sets me to fly high
like the bird of spring
returning.

Another love song

I never knew
that joy
could come from such
simple things

Yet here I stand
hand in my hair
and the other
to cover my mouth

You just passed by
but then you stopped
and smiled
with twinkling eye

Piraeus

I bite the sensuous flesh
of the ripe fig
while cicadas bid
endlessly
like old women
who dig at my early grave
and I think of you:
Your warm body

The sun bleaches stone
and heat fades
the blues
to grey
while old women pull at me
with their ancient and tired
morality
and I think of you: Your hot breath.

When the jasmine
sweetens the air
and scrawny cats
leap from too insistent a stare
I lie
bathing in sweat
with the cooing of the dove
reminding me of love:
Your moist lips.

Hope

How life can spring

from dead seeds

never

ceases to amaze

Transmigrator

When,
      On one of those rare
      blue days
      a lazy haze
      would mesmerize
      the tender skies
      my heart dared
      to be
      the roving rambler.

Then,
      Far from home
      in search of the drab and grizzle
      with winds to whip up the drizzle
      like some homing pigeon
      it trills and strains
      to see the red-tiled roofs
      under the splashing rains.

And yet again,
      with throbbing wing
      it sinks to find
      the drift
      of the west-ward wind.

www.ingramcontent.com/pod-product-compliance
Lightning Source LLC
LaVergne TN
LVHW011414080426
835511LV00005B/542